STAR WARS

What is a Wookiee?
and Other Adventures

LONDON, NEW YORK,
MELBOURNE, MUNICH, and DELHI

Editorial Lead Heather Jones
Senior Production Editor Clare McLean
Production Editor Kavita Varma
Managing Editor Catherine Saunders
Managing Art Editor Ron Stobbart
Brand Manager Lisa Lanzarini
Publishing Manager Simon Beecroft
Category Publisher Alex Allan
Production Controller Katherine Whyte

Lucasfilm
Executive Editor Jonathan W. Rinzler
Art Director Troy Alders
Continuity Supervisor Leland Chee
Reading Consultant Linda B. Gambrell, Ph.D.
004-180393-Oct/10

This edition published in Canada in 2010
Dorling Kindersley is represented in Canada by
Tourmaline Editions Inc
662 King Street West
Suite 304 Toronto, Ontario M5V 1M7

First published in the United States in 2005–2010 as
six separate titles: *Star Wars: Ready Set Podrace 2007, Star
Wars: Luke Skywalker's Amazing Story 2009, Star Wars:
What is a Wookiee? 2005, Star Wars: Journey Through
Space 2005, Star Wars: A Queen's Diary 2007, Star Wars:
R2–D2 and Friends 2009*

ISBN: 978-1-55363-151-4

Printed and bound in China by L Rex Printing Co., Ltd.

**Discover more at
www.dk.com**

www.starwars.com

STAR WARS

WHAT IS A WOOKIEE?

AND OTHER ADVENTURES

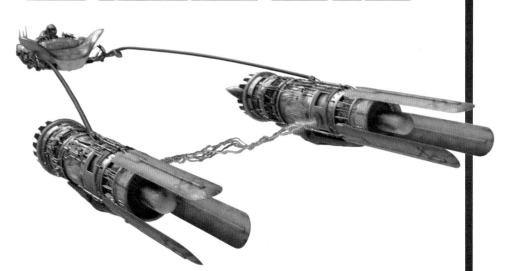

DK

Contents

Ready, Set, Podrace! 5

Luke Skywalker's Amazing Story 35

What is a Wookiee? 65

Journey Through Space 95

A Queen's Diary 125

R2-D2 and Friends 155

STAR WARS

READY, SET, PODRACE!

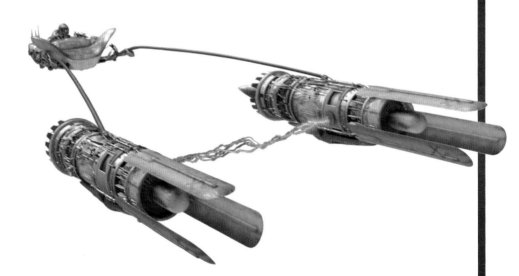

Written by Simon Beecroft

Do you like fast races?

Would you like to see
the fastest race ever?

A Podrace is the fastest race
you will ever see!

In a Podrace, each pilot flies
a machine called a Podracer.

Podracers fly just above
the ground.

Podracers fly very fast!

Podracer

Podracer pilots sit
in a seat called
a cockpit.

Cockpit

All the driving controls
are in front of them.

The pilots have to move
the controls very quickly
when they are racing.

Do you think you could fly
a Podracer?

This desert racetrack has lots of twists and turns.
Some of these twists and turns are very dangerous.

The pilot who
reaches the end
of the race first
is the winner.

Racetrack

Many people come to watch
the Podraces.
The people shout and cheer.

14

They are excited to see the race.
They want to find out
which racer will win.

Podracing is very dangerous.

The pilots fly along at really
fast speeds.

Some racers crash into each other, and some racers crash into cliffs.

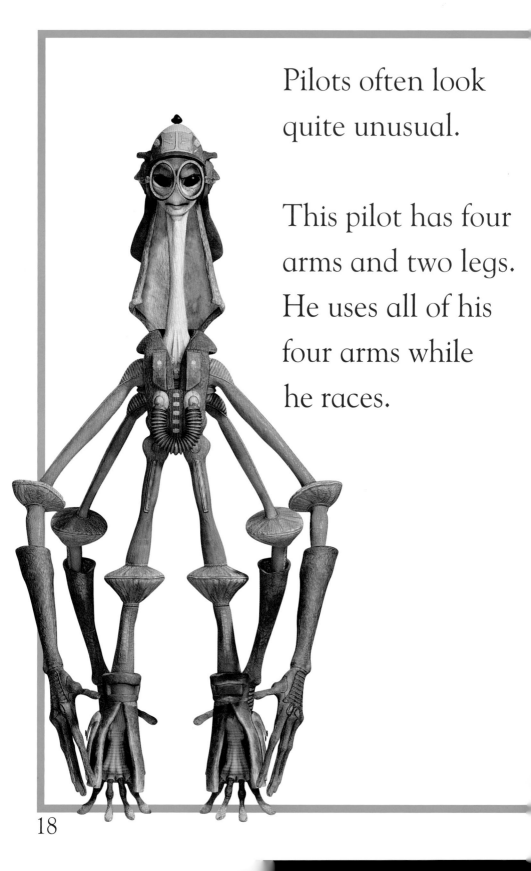

Pilots often look quite unusual.

This pilot has four arms and two legs. He uses all of his four arms while he races.

18

This pilot has three eyes.
His extra eye helps him
spot dangers in the race.

This pilot is wearing goggles.
They are special racing goggles.
His racing goggles
protect his eyes
from the desert sand.

This pilot is nervous.
He is worried because
his Podracer is broken.
He will not finish the race.

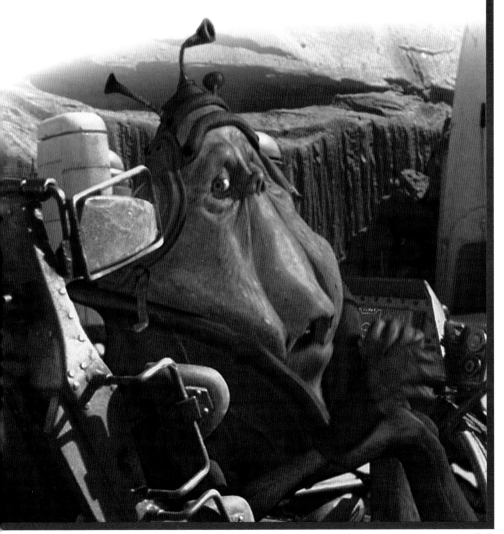

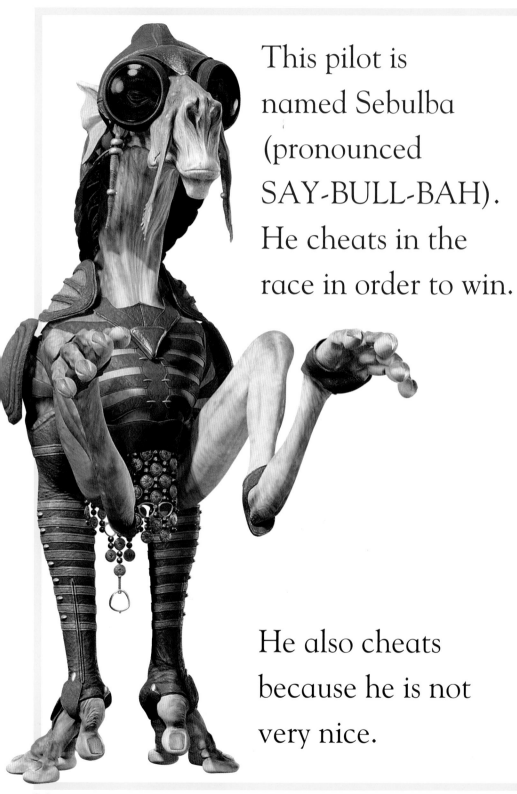

This pilot is
named Sebulba
(pronounced
SAY-BULL-BAH).
He cheats in the
race in order to win.

He also cheats
because he is not
very nice.

Sebulba sometimes throws
his tools at the
other pilots.
He wants to
force them out
of the race.

Tools

Selbulba is a very
dangerous
racer.

Pilots prepare their machines
for the race in a big garage
called a hangar.

Robots clean
the Podracers and
repair the engines.

Each pilot makes
sure his Podracer
is ready to go!

Engines

Today is one of
the most exciting
Podraces ever.

It is exciting
because one of
the racers is
a young boy.
The boy is
named Anakin
(AN-NA-KIN).

Anakin has never finished
a Podrace before.

Anakin built his Podracer all by himself.

He is only nine years old,
but he is a very good pilot.

Anakin's family and friends are
going to watch him race.

The pilots are on the starting line.
Ready, set,
Podrace!

The race is very exciting.
Sebulba does everything he can
to win.
He tries to push Anakin out
of the race.

Anakin is a better racer
than Sebulba.
Sebulba crashes!

Anakin wins the race.
Anakin's friends and family are
very happy, but Anakin is
happiest of all!

Glossary

Cockpit a space that a pilot sits in

Engines machines that make a vehicle move

Podracer a vehicle that flies close to the ground

Racetrack an oval piece of track that vehicles race on

Tools items that are used for mechanical work

STAR WARS

LUKE SKYWALKER'S
AMAZING STORY

Written by Simon Beecroft

This is Luke.

He dreams of having adventures.

He lives on a far away planet with his aunt and uncle.

His aunt and uncle are called...

Aunt Beru and Uncle Owen.

Uncle Owen is a farmer.

He buys two droids to help him on his farm.

The droids are called...

C-3PO and R2-D2.

R2-D2 has a secret message for a strange old man who lives nearby.

Luke watches the message.

The old man is called...

Obi-Wan Kenobi.

Obi-Wan Kenobi is a Jedi.
He knew Luke's father.

Luke has never met his father.

Luke's father is called...

Anakin Skywalker.

Anakin Skywalker was once a Jedi, like Obi-Wan Kenobi.

But Anakin turned to the dark side of the Force.

Then he became
known as...

Darth Vader.

Darth Vader wants to rule
the galaxy.

Some people want to stop him.

They are called Rebels.

Darth Vader has captured the
leader of the Rebels.

She is called...

Princess Leia.

Princess Leia put the message inside R2-D2 for Obi-Wan Kenobi. She needs Obi-Wan's help.

Obi-Wan takes Luke to meet two pilots.

The pilots are called...

Han Solo and Chewbacca.

They have a fast spaceship.
Obi-Wan asks Han Solo if he will
fly them into space.

Han Solo says he will. So...

Chewbacca, Luke, Obi-Wan, Han Solo, C-3PO, and R2-D2 all fly in the fast spaceship to a big space station called the Death Star.

Some soldiers try
to capture them.
The soldiers
are called...

Stormtroopers.

They are Darth Vader's soldiers.
Luke, Han, and Chewbacca fight
the Stormtroopers.

They rescue Princess Leia.
They take Leia to...

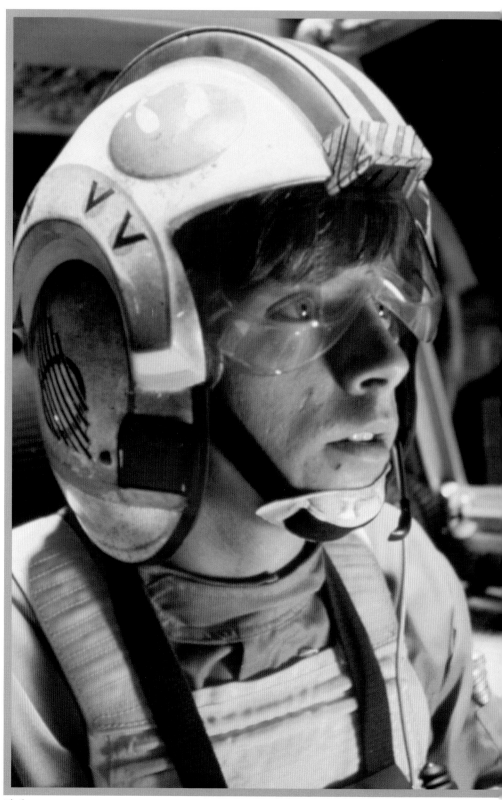

The Rebels.

The Rebels attack the Death Star in their spaceships.

Luke blows up the Death Star with a very lucky shot.

Later Luke visits...

Yoda.

Yoda is a Jedi. He lives in a swamp.

Yoda trains Luke to be a Jedi.
Luke realizes it is time to meet...

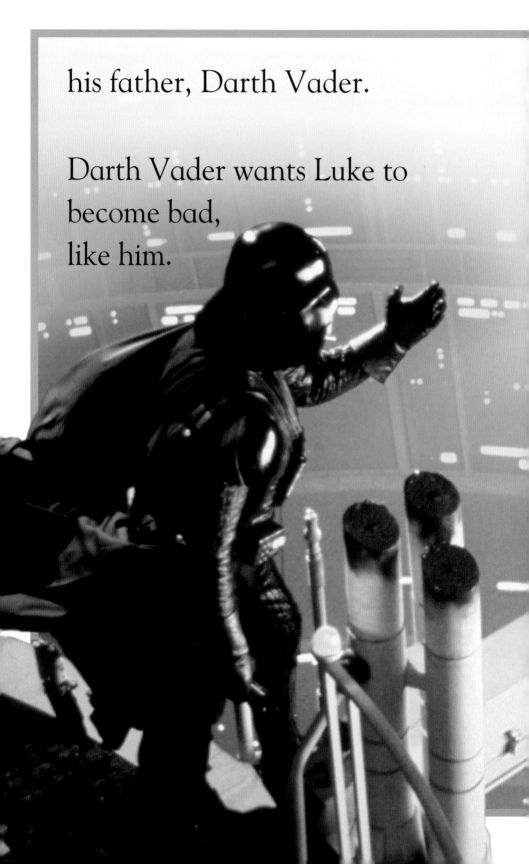

his father, Darth Vader.

Darth Vader wants Luke to
become bad,
like him.

In the end, Luke
helps Darth
Vader become
good again.

Darth Vader
turns back into...

61

Anakin Skywalker, Luke's real father.

Luke takes off Darth Vader's helmet. Luke looks at his father's face.

He is happy to see his father at last.

Quiz!

1. Who is Luke's father?

2. What is this droid's name?

3. Who is this?

4. Who teaches Luke to be a Jedi?

Answers: 1. Anakin Skywalker, 2. C-3PO, 3. Princess Leia, 4. Yoda

STAR WARS

WHAT IS A WOOKIEE?

Written by Laura Buller and Kate Simkins

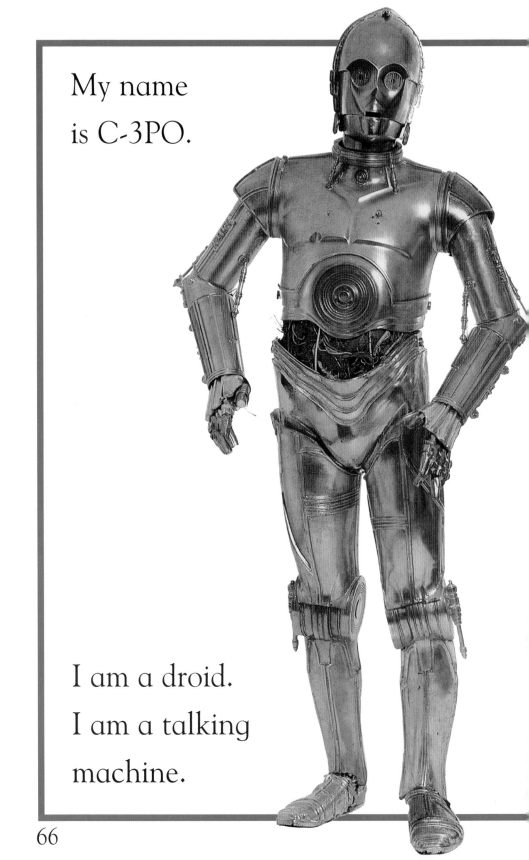

My name
is C-3PO.

I am a droid.
I am a talking
machine.

I live far, far away in space.
Lots of creatures live here.
I will be telling you
about some of them.

Space

Some creatures in *Star Wars*
are aliens.

Aliens are not human.
There are lots of different aliens.

Humans also live here—
my friend Padmé (PAD-MAY) is
a human.

This is my friend R2-D2.
He is a droid too.

R2-D2 likes talking.
His voice sounds like
whistles and beeps, but
I can understand him.

R2-D2 is a clever
little machine.
He has all sorts
of useful tools.
He can fix anything!

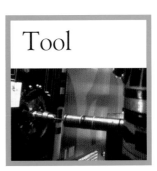

Tool

Meet Chewbacca.

He is a tall,
furry alien
called
a Wookiee.

He is the best friend of Han Solo, who is a human.
They fly a spaceship together.

Sometimes,
I ride with them!

Spaceship

Now say hello
to Jar Jar Binks.

He is a friendly
alien.

Jar Jar comes from
an underwater city.
On land, Jar Jar is always
falling over!

He uses his long tongue
to catch food to eat.

Let's visit Watto's shop.

Watto is a blue alien.
He has a bad temper.
Watto flies about
using the wings on his back.

He sells bits of old machines
called junk.

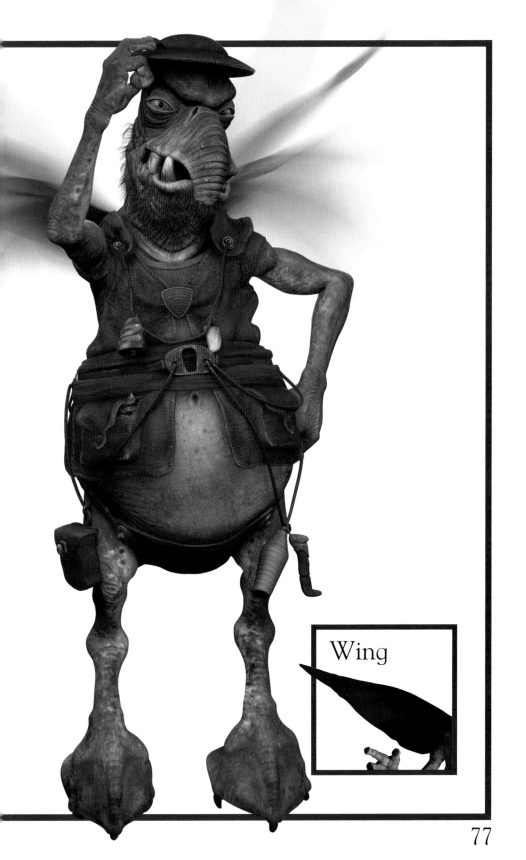

Wing

Now it's time
to meet Sebulba
(SEE-BUL-BAH).

This nasty alien
races in a vehicle
called a Podracer.
He likes to go fast.

Podracer

Sebulba will do anything to win.
He will even throw things
at other Podracers!

Pit droids fix the Podracers.
They are very useful and
can carry heavy things.

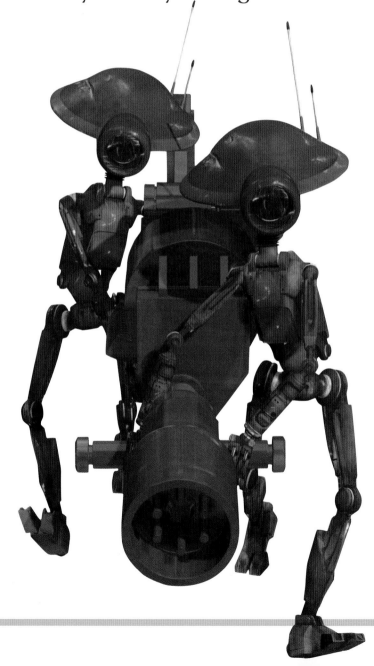

Pit droids sometimes
get into trouble.
There is one way to stop them.
Tap them on the nose
and they fold up.

Jabba the Hutt is a nasty alien.
He has a fat body and a long tail.
His body is covered in sticky slime.

Tail

Jabba's eyes are red and yellow
and his breath is smelly.
Don't get too near him!

Let's visit Dexter Jettster's
restaurant.

This friendly alien has four arms.
He cooks the food at Dexter's Diner

Dexter knows lots of things.

What shall we ask him?

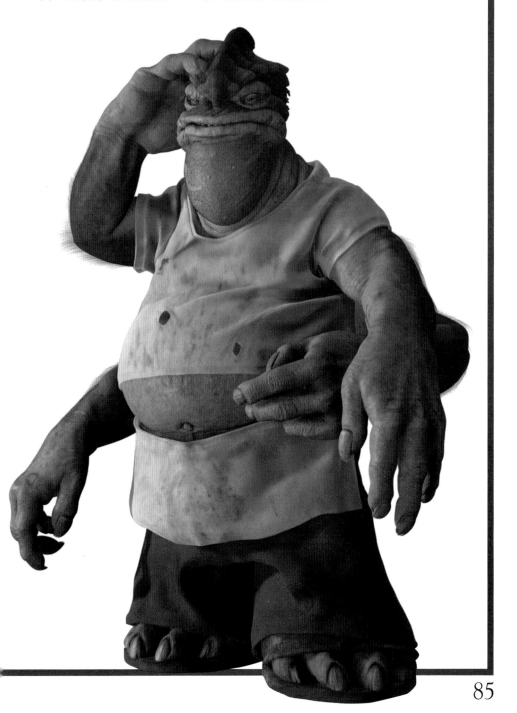

These creatures
are lizard keepers.

They live
in big holes
in the ground.

Sometimes, the lizard keepers ride around on giant lizards. The lizards are good at jumping and climbing.

Jawas are small creatures
with shiny yellow eyes.

Their faces
are hidden under
the hoods of
their brown cloaks.

Hood

These little aliens
find droids and
bits of machines to sell.

Once, they even sold
R2-D2!

If we go deep into the forest,
we may meet the Ewoks.

Ewoks are small, furry creatures.
They live in houses
that they build high up
in the trees.

Forest

91

Yoda is very old and very wise.
He has green skin and
big, pointy ears.

No one knows what kind
of creature he is or
where he comes from.

I hope you have enjoyed learning about the creatures in *Star Wars*.

Goodbye!

Picture Word List

Space

page 5

Podracer

page 17

Tool

page 9

Tail

page 20

Spaceship

page 11

Hood

page 26

Wing

page 15

Forest

page 29

STAR WARS
Journey Through
SPACE

Written by Ryder Windham

Come on a journey through space
to the *Star Wars* galaxy.
It is far, far away.
In this galaxy, there are
many stars and planets.

Coruscant (CORE-RUS-SANT)
is the most important planet.
It is covered by one enormous city.
All the buildings in the city
are gleaming skyscrapers.

Jedi Knights

Many creatures live in
the *Star Wars* galaxy.
Coruscant is the home
of powerful warriors
called Jedi Knights.

Yoda

People and Gungans live on
the planet Naboo.
The people live in beautiful cities
on the land.
Young Padmé Amidala was once
Queen of Naboo.

Queen
Amidala

The Gungans live
in underwater cities.
They can walk
on land too,
although some are
a bit clumsy!
Jar Jar Binks
is a Gungan.

*Jar Jar
Binks*

Podracing

Tatooine is famous
for Podracing.
In this dangerous sport,
fast vehicles race each
other through the desert.

The planet Tatooine (TA-TOO-EEN)
is covered by a dusty desert.
Two suns shine in the sky so
it is very hot.
Tatooine is a meeting place.
Space travellers visit the planet from
all over the galaxy.

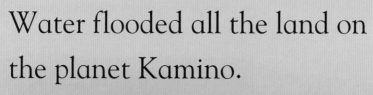
Water flooded all the land on
the planet Kamino.
So the Kaminoans built their cities
on strong metal poles that stick up
above the water.

Kaminoans are very tall
with long, thin necks.
They ride winged beasts
to fly and swim around
their watery planet.

Geonosis (GEE-OH-NO-SIS) is
not a good place to be captured.
Prisoners are forced to fight huge
monsters in special arenas.

Huge arenas
The arenas are
made of rock.
There are lots
of seats inside.

Scary beasts are brought from other planets to the arenas.
The Geonosians look like insects and enjoy watching the fights.

Chewbacca

Tarfful

Kashyyyk (KASH-ICK) is a world
of giant trees and shallow lakes.
It is home to the Wookiees,
including Chewbacca and Tarfful.
Wookiees are tall and have lots
of shaggy fur.
They talk in grunts and roars.

Good friends
Chewbacca is friends
with a human
called Han Solo.
They fly together
in a starship – the
Millennium Falcon.

The planet Utapau
(OO-TA-POW)
has lots of deep holes.
The Utapauns dig
tunnels through
the rocks to join
the holes.

There are other
creatures on
the planet.

An Utapaun

Creatures called Utai (OO-TIE) live in holes in the ground.

Enormous varactyl (VA-RACK-TILL) wander around the rocky land. They are good climbers.

An Utai

The Utai ride the varactyl.

A varactyl

The red planet of Mustafar

(MUSS-TAH-FAR) is

a very hot place.

It is covered in fiery volcanoes.

Hot, melted rock called lava

flows from the volcanoes.

The sky is filled with black smoke

that blocks out the sun.

Fight on Mustafar

Two Jedi Knights, Obi-Wan Kenobi and Anakin Skywalker, fought each other on Mustafar.

Anakin had turned from good to evil. Obi-Wan won the fight.

The space rock known as
Polis Massa (POE-LISS-MASS-AH)
has a medical center.
This is where space travelers can go
if they are sick.

The doctors are helped
by special robots
called droids.

Medical droid

Polis Massa doctors

Birth place
Padmé Amidala came to Polis Massa to give birth. She had twins.

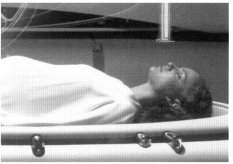

The moon Yavin 4 is covered
in thick jungle.
The ruins of very old buildings
called temples rise above the trees.

At one time, the soldiers
who lived on Yavin 4 kept watch
for enemy starships from
the tops of the tallest temples.

What's inside the temples?

The temples were once used to keep starships. There were also rooms where people could eat and sleep.

The ice planet Hoth
is so cold that people can
freeze to death there.

On Hoth, people ride around on
large beasts called tauntauns.

Wampa ice creatures
live in ice caves.
They hang
the animals that
they catch from
the cave roof.

One time, a wampa even captured
a Jedi Knight!

The planet Dagobah (DAY-GO-BA) is covered in thick forests and swampy land.

The air is steamy, and it rains a lot.

There are many deadly creatures and poisonous plants.

The Jedi Master Yoda went
to hide on Dagobah.
He lived in a small tree house.

Crash landing

Young pilot
Luke Skywalker
crashed his
starship on
Dagobah.
Yoda found Luke
and took him to
his tiny house.

Cloud City floats in the skies of
the planet Bespin.

Visitors come to enjoy
its lively shops, restaurants,
and hotels.

A cloud car

Cloud cars fly around the city.
They have room for two passengers.

The forest moon of
the planet Endor is
the home of small, furry
creatures called Ewoks.
They live in the trees and
use simple tools and spears.

At night, Ewoks stay in the villages that they build high up in the trees.

We hope that you have enjoyed your trip to the *Star Wars* galaxy. Come back soon!

Fascinating facts

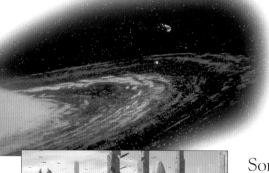

There are millions and millions of planets and suns in the enormous *Star Wars* galaxy.

Some of the skyscrapers on Coruscant are nearly a mile high.

The Queen of Naboo lives in the Royal Palace. This beautiful building has large windows and polished stone floors.

The trees on Kashyyyk are very tall. The Wookiees make houses in the trees.

The tauntauns have thick gray fur to protect them from the cold on Hoth.

STAR WARS
A Queen's Diary

Written by Simon Beecroft

My name is Padmé Amidala.

I am the Queen of my planet.

Today I am going to start a diary.

I am going to start a diary because my life is very busy.

I do not want to forget anything.

My world

If people read this diary in the future, they might not know about my world. So I am going to explain interesting things about my world in these boxes.

Today I tried to count all the rooms
in the palace, where I live.
I quickly lost count.
My palace is so large I think I shall
never be able to explore all of it.

I love to climb up to one of the highest rooms.

Then I gaze at the waterfalls that flow down the side of the mountain.

Home world

I live on a planet called Naboo.
Naboo is a small planet.
It is very beautiful.

Today a lot of important people visited me.

When people meet me, some of them are surprised that I am so young.

I am just 14 years old.

All queens on my planet are young.

I am not even the youngest!

Even though I am not very old, I want to be a good queen.

Landspeeder

This morning I flew in a landspeeder.
I love travelling fast in landspeeders.
I flew around the city and looked at
all the pretty buildings.
Lots of people waved at me.

My palace is in the biggest city
on Naboo, but I have not always
lived here.

I was born in a mountain village.

People of Naboo

The humans who
live on my planet
are called the Naboo.
I am one of them.
The Naboo live in
cities and villages.

I was learning about the Gungans
in my lessons today.
I learned that the Gungans also
live on my planet.
They live in underwater cities.
The Gungans can also live on land.
I would like to meet a Gungan.

Naboo natives

The Naboo and the Gungans do not often meet each other. They are not enemies, but they are not friends either!

Gungan   *Naboo*

I often think about my
parents and sisters.
I have many memories
of growing up
in my village.

When I was young,
my teachers realized
I was very clever.
My teachers gave me
extra training.
Later, people
decided to vote for
me as Queen.
It was the proudest
day of my life!

Padmé

Ruwee

Sola

Jobal

Eirtaé

Rabé

I have handmaidens who look
after me and help me dress.
They also protect me from danger.

My handmaidens are my friends, too.
Eirtaé (pronounced AIR-TAY)
and Rabé are two of my
closest handmaidens.

Royal dress
On my planet,
kings and queens
wear special clothes
and makeup.
They also wear their
hair in special ways.

Today I am going to visit a nearby planet in my special spaceship. My spaceship is totally silver.

Spaceships

Naboo kings and queens fly silver spaceships. There is even a throne in my ship!

It has large rooms inside.

No one has a spaceship like mine.

I am even learning to fly it.

Sabé

Sometimes it is hard being Queen,
because everyone knows me.
Sabé is my best friend
and one of my handmaidens.

Padmé

Sometimes Sabé dresses as me,
and I dress as a handmaiden.
We have a secret way of talking
in code when we are in disguise.

A terrible thing has happened.
My planet has been invaded.
Enemy soldiers tried to capture me,
but I was saved by two Jedi Knights.
I had never met a Jedi before,
but I had heard about them.
They travel everywhere to help
people in need.

Droid soldiers

The enemy soldiers are machines called droids. Every droid soldier is armed and dangerous.

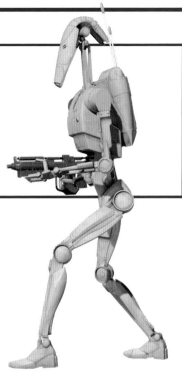

Now we are flying away from my planet to search for help for my people.

We have landed on a planet
to repair the spaceship.
The planet is rough and dry.
We went to a local town.
I went in disguise so no one
would know I was a queen.
I met a boy who is a slave.
This means that someone
owns him, and he is not free
to ever leave his master.

This young boy is very special.

His name is Anakin.

He told me I looked like an angel.

I think we will be friends.

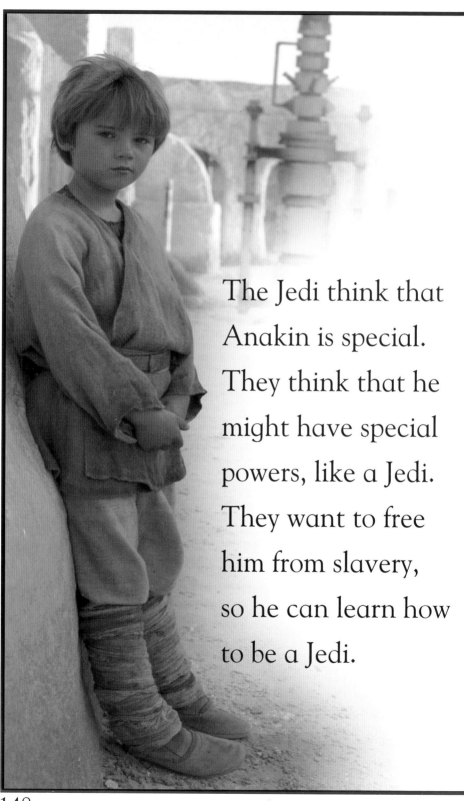

The Jedi think that
Anakin is special.
They think that he
might have special
powers, like a Jedi.
They want to free
him from slavery,
so he can learn how
to be a Jedi.

Amazing news! Anakin is free!
He won a dangerous race in his
Podracer to gain his freedom.
Now we can get help for my planet.

Amazing machines

Anakin has built many clever things.
He built a walking machine called
a droid and a racing machine
called a Podracer.

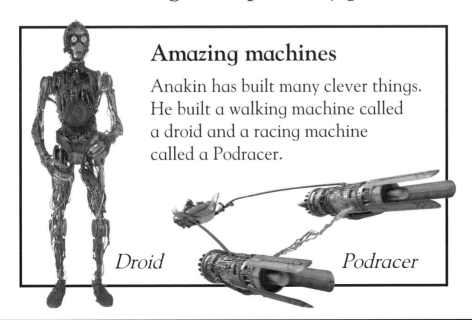

Droid

Podracer

Today I became a fighter.
No one would help my people,
so I had to help them myself.
I went with the Jedi to ask the
Gungans for help.

Together we made an army
and fought the enemy droid soldiers.
The Gungans fought bravely,
but many of them died.

Weapons

The Gungans use many weapons in battle, including giant catapults.

My planet is free!

Anakin helped us a lot.

He flew a spaceship straight into the
invaders' spaceship and blew it up!
Although it was really an accident,
when Anakin destroyed the ship the
droids could no longer fight.

Now I'm sure Anakin
will be trained as a Jedi.

Perhaps we will
meet again....

Places I have visited

I traveled to the swamps on my planet. The Gungans have a secret meeting place there.

I visited a dangerous planet called Tatooine with the Jedi Qui-Gon Jinn. We went to a busy town.

When I was visiting Tatooine, I watched a fast sporting race called a Podrace. A huge crowd gathered to watch the race.

I flew to the center of the galaxy to visit the capital planet. One enormous city covers the entire planet.

STAR WARS

R2-D2
AND FRIENDS

Written by Simon Beecroft

R2-D2

R2-D2

This is R2-D2. He is a clever machine called a droid.

R2-D2 talks using whistles and beeps. He can talk to other droids, and some humans can understand him as well.

R2-D2 is not very big, but he is no pushover. When he is angry, he bounces up and down and stamps his feet!

Droid height

R2-D2 is just under one meter tall. He's only a little bit shorter than Anakin when he was a young boy.

Droid Jobs

R2-D2 is an astromech droid. Astromech droids take care of spaceships. Sometimes they help human pilots fly spaceships, too.

R2-D2 helped Anakin to fly this spaceship

R2-D2 can talk to computers that help fly the spaceships. He plugs a special tool into the computer to talk to it.

R2-D2 has lots of tools hidden inside his body. So don't be surprised if a cutting arm or a grasping arm pops out of a panel in his body.

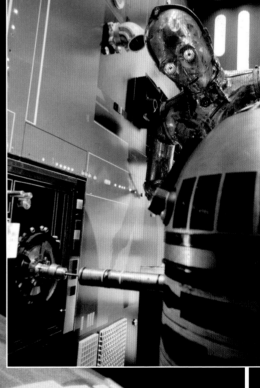

Special Powers

R2-D2 moves around on his three wheeled feet.

R2-D2 can fly as well. He uses rocket boosters that pop out of his sides.

Secret message

R2-D2 can record and play messages. Here's Princess Leia, who recorded a secret message for Obi-Wan Kenobi.

R2-D2 can look around corners or from underwater using a special eye that pops up from the top of his head.

Deadly Missions

R2-D2's life is very exciting.

He once repaired Padmé Amidala's

spaceship from the outside while it

was flying in space.

Owners

R2-D2 has worked for
Padmé Amidala, Anakin
Skywalker, Princess Leia,
and Luke Skywalker.

Another time, some Jawas captured R2-D2. The Jawas sold R2-D2 to Owen Lars, Luke Skywalker's uncle.

R4-G9   R5-X2   R4-A22

Astromech Droids

Astromech droids like R2-D2 come in all sorts of colors and styles.

R2-D2 used to work with a team of astromech droids in Padmé Amidala's spaceship.

R4-P17 had a red dome. It was built into Obi-Wan Kenobi's spaceship. Unfortunately a nasty buzz droid destroyed R4-P17 in a big space battle.

Uncle Owen nearly bought a droid called R5-D4. But it was faulty and its head blew up. So Owen chose trusty R2-D2 instead.

R5-D4

C-3PO

R2-D2 is best friends with a golden droid called C-3PO. R2-D2 is scared of nothing, but C-3PO worries about everything!

C-3PO is a protocol droid. Protocol droids can speak millions of languages. They help people in the galaxy speak to each other.

See-through PO!

Anakin Skywalker built C-3PO. At first, C-3PO was not covered in shiny golden metal. You could see all his wires and parts. C-3PO said that he felt naked!

Clumsy Droid

Parts of C-3PO's body would sometimes fall off. Luckily, it doesn't hurt him and he can be repaired.

Once, a big machine in a factory pulled off C-3PO's head by mistake. The machine put a different head onto his body. Fortunately, R2-D2 came to C-3PO's rescue!

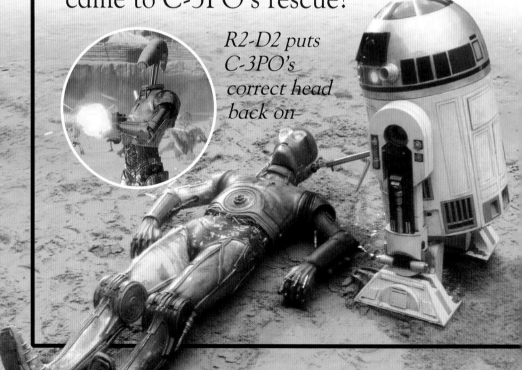

R2-D2 puts C-3PO's correct head back on

Another time, C-3PO was completely taken apart.

If it hadn't been for his friend Chewbacca, he'd have been recycled!

Clean machine

C-3PO loves to soak in an oil bath. It cleans off all the dust and dirt from his parts and makes him feel like new again.

Famous Adventures

C-3PO and R2-D2 have had lots of adventures together!

They once traveled to Jabba the Hutt's palace to rescue their friend Han Solo. But Jabba captured them. Jabba forced C-3PO to become his translator droid. Poor R2-D2 became a waiter, with a drinks tray attached to his head!

On another mission, C-3PO met the furry Ewoks, who live in tree houses. The Ewoks thought that such a shiny droid must have great magical powers!

Protocol Droids

Most protocol droids are friendly, but some are dangerous.

TC-14 tried to trick Qui-Gon Jinn and Obi-Wan Kenobi. He led them into a room that filled with poisonous gas. The Jedi escaped, but they let TC-14 go.

TC-14 looks like C-3PO, but she is silver not gold

4-LOM has a body like C-3PO, but his head is shaped like an insect's head. His job is to capture people. Darth Vader

4-LOM

once wanted him to find and capture Han Solo.

CZ-3

CZ-3 was an unlucky droid. He got mixed up in one of Jabba the Hutt's criminal plots. He was destroyed and scrap dealers stole his remains.

Droids Everywhere

Droids are everywhere. They do all sorts of jobs.

This gatekeeper droid stands inside the door at Jabba's palace. When visitors knock, it pokes its eye through a peep-hole in the door.

Gonk, gonk! What's that noise? It's a GNK droid, also called a gonk droid. Gonk droids walk around on two legs and supply power to machines.

Gonk droid

Watch out for MSE-6 droids, also called mouse droids. These small cleaning and repair droids whiz by your feet—don't trip over one!

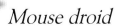

Mouse droid

Medical Droids

If you are ill or hurt, you might need a medical droid to take care of you!

A team of medical droids rebuilt Darth Vader's body after he was hurt in a fight with Obi-Wan Kenobi. They fitted black armor and a black helmet onto his body.

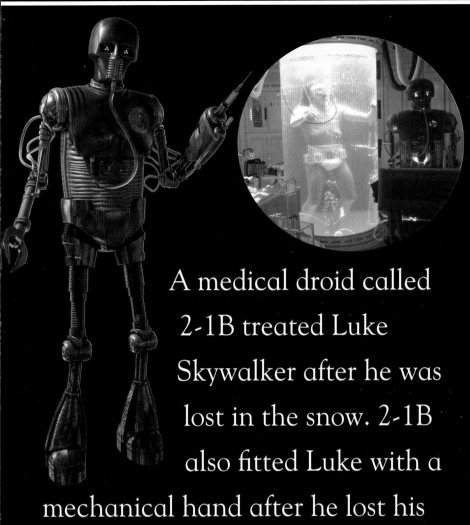

A medical droid called 2-1B treated Luke Skywalker after he was lost in the snow. 2-1B also fitted Luke with a mechanical hand after he lost his own in a fight with Darth Vader.

Midwife droids

These droids helped Padmé Amidala give birth to Luke and Leia.

Deadly Droids

Some droids are not friendly. They have blasters and other deadly weapons.

Droidekas roll into battle like a ball. Then they unwind and shield

Battle droid

themselves in glowing energy. They have blasters on both arms.

Droideka

Spider droids walk on four legs. Their dome-shaped heads are

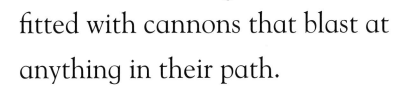

Spider droid

fitted with cannons that blast at anything in their path.

Droid starfighters can fly in space, with their guns blazing. They can also walk into battle on the tips of their wings. Either way, watch out!

Spy Droids

Spy droids might be watching you so beware!

Darth Maul's spy droids fly around looking for Queen Amidala, Jedi Qui-Gon Jinn, and Obi-Wan Kenobi.

Spy droid

Darth Vader used probe droids to look for his enemies. Han Solo destroyed this one with his blaster!

Imperial droids

Little patrol droids are everywhere, looking for criminals. They report to Stormtroopers.

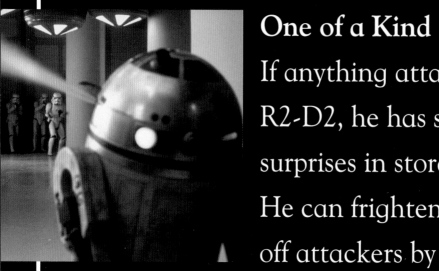

One of a Kind

If anything attacks R2-D2, he has some surprises in store! He can frighten off attackers by shooting out jets of smoke and making loud noises and whistles.

Once he destroyed a deadly buzz droid that attacked Anakin Skywalker's spaceship!

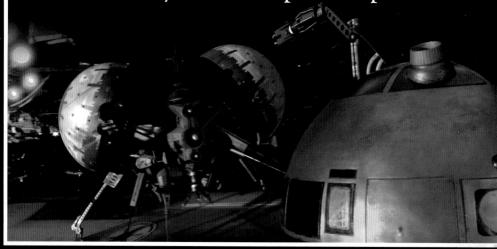

But R2-D2 won't frighten you.
You are one of his friends. Listen.
"Beep whoot ooo!"
R2-D2 is saying goodbye to you.

Goodbye R2-D2!

Test your Knowledge

Which of these droids are friendly and which are not?

Good ☐   Bad ☐

Good ☐   Bad ☐

Good ☐   Bad ☐

Good ☐   Bad ☐

Index

Anakin Skywalker 26–29, 31–33, 44, 62, 111, 147–149, 153, 156, 162, 167, 182
astromech droid 158, 184

Bespin 120
binks, Jar Jar 99
buzz droid 165, 182

C-3PO 40, 52, 167, 168, 169, 170, 171, 172, 173
Chewbacca 50, 52, 55, 72, 106, 107, 169
Coruscant 97, 124

Dagobah 118, 119
Darth Maul 180
Darth Vader 46, 47, 55, 60, 61, 62, 176, 177, 181
Death Star 52, 57
droid soldiers 145, 151, 153
droid starfighters 179
droids 39, 40

Eirtaé 138, 139
Endor 122
Ewoks 122, 123, 171

Force, The 44

Geonosians 104, 105
Gungans 134, 135, 150, 151

handmaidens 139, 142, 143
Hoth 116, 124

Jabba the Hutt 170, 173, 174
Jawas 163
Jedi 43, 44, 58, 59, 144, 148, 150, 153
Jobal Amidala 37

Kaminoans 102, 103
Kashyyyk 107, 124
Kenobi, Obi-Wan 111

Luke Skywalker 119, 162, 163
medical droid 176, 177
Mustafar 110, 111

Naboo 98, 124, 129, 133, 135
Obi-Wan Kenobi 43, 44, 48, 51, 52, 161, 165, 172, 176, 180
Owen Lars 163, 165

Padmé Amidala 98, 113, 126, 136, 162, 164, 177, 180
pilot 10, 11, 12, 16–25
planet 126, 129, 131, 133, 134, 139, 140, 144–146, 149, 153
Podrace 7, 8, 14, 26, 27, 30
Princess Leia 48, 55, 161, 177

Queen 126, 131, 136, 139, 140, 142, 146
Qui-Gon Jinn 172, 180

R2-D2 8, 40, 48, 52, 156–183
Rabé 138, 139
race 6, 7, 13, 14, 21–24, 31, 33
racer 15, 17, 23, 33
racetrack 12, 13
Rebels 47, 57
Ruwee Amidala 137

Sabé 142, 143
Sola Amidala 137
Solo, Han 107
spaceship 140, 141, 146, 150, 152, 153, 157, 158, 164, 182

Tarfful 106, 107
tauntauns 116, 124

wampa ice creatures 117
Wookies 66–94, 107, 124

Yavin 96, 114
Yoda 58, 59, 97, 119